AN ALPHABET OF SAINTS

Rhymed by

Robert Hugh Benson
Reginald Balfour: Charles Ritchie

Drawn by

Lindsay Symington

This book is a reproduction of the original 1905
impression made by Burns and Oates, London, England

Neumann Press

Charlotte, North Carolina

CATHOLIC BOOK PUBLISHERS
www.NeumannPress.com

This book is a reproduction of the original 1905 impression made by Burns and Oates, London, England.

Published by Neumann Press, an imprint of TAN Books.

ISBN: 978-1-930873-12-4

Printed and bound in the United States of America.

Neumann Press
Charlotte, North Carolina
www.NeumannPress.com
2014

THE DEDICATION

R.B. C.R. et R.H.B.
Filiolae CLARAE ANGELAE
Hoc Alphabetum dono dant
PIOQUE PAPAE DEDICANT

THE PREFACE

THE twenty-six SAINTS in this volume of rhymes
Lived in various places at various times;
But now they're together in Heaven, and know
All we think, say and do in the world here below;
And since all that you ask—if you pray for good ends—
Will be granted by GOD at the prayer of His friends,
You should call on these SAINTS in the days of your youth
For the Peace of the Church and the Triumph of Truth.
We hope, as these Rhymes are the best we can do,
That the SAINTS will be pleased, and that you'll be pleased too.

SAINT ANTONY *of* PADUA, *Confessor, Friar Minor of
the Order of Saint Francis of Assisi. Born in Portugal,
1196; Died at Padua, 1231; Feast, June 13.*

St ANTONY *of* PADUA

A is ANTONY of PADUA, a Friar wise and kind ;
He never had a penny, but he never seemed to mind ;
He was very fond of reading, but the book he read the most
Was the book that tells of GOD, the Father, Son and Holy Ghost;
He was very fond of children, but the Child he loved the best
Was the little Infant JESUS, as He lay on Mary's breast ;
And once when he was reading with the Gospel on a stand
Little JESUS stood upon it and caressed him with His hand.
  Now that ANTONY'S in Heaven, if you ever lose your toys,
  I advise you to invoke him, for he's good to girls and boys.

SAINT BENEDICT, *Abbot, Patriarch of all Western Monks, Founder of the Order called Benedictine; Born at Nursia, in Italy, 480; Died at Monte Cassino, 543. Feast, March 21.*

St BENEDICT

B for SAINT BENEDICT, Hermit and Sage,
Whose Rule has been kept by most Monks since his age.
Cyrilla, his Governess, took him from home
To learn how to read at a day-school in Rome,
Where he went to his lessons with satchel and pen
And rode back by the Tiber to supper again.
He loved contemplation so much that one day
He agreed with Cyrilla to run right away ;
And for years in the mountains he fasted and prayed
Till the praise of the neighbours made BENET afraid ;
So he wandered and wandered, but stayed in the end
In a cave near ROMANUS the Monk, his good friend.
Before long many Monks gathered round him to pray,
And his Rule and his Monks are still mighty to-day.
O Blessed Saint BENET, I wish I could be
Half as good for one year as you were sixty-three.

SAINT CHRISTOPHER, *Martyr; Born in the Holy Land;*
· Martyred at Samos, in Lycia, 364. Feast, July 25.

St CHRISTOPHER

C for SAINT CHRISTOPHER, loved of the LORD,
Who lived all alone in a hut by a ford;
When travellers came there by night or by day,
He carried them over and showed them the way.
One night when the weather was wintry and wild,
He heard his name called by the voice of a child:
"O CHRISTOPHER, carry me, carry me home:
O Christopher, Christopher, Christopher, come."
The Saint was surprised when the crossing began
To find Him as heavy as any grown man;
And when they were over he found to his joy
It was CHRIST he had carried instead of a boy.

SAINT DOMINIC, *Confessor; Founder of the Order of Preachers, or Preaching Friars, called in Latin Dominicani after him (Domini Canes is Latin for Hounds of the Lord); Born in Spain, 1170; Died at Bologna, in Italy, August 6, 1221, Feast, August 4.*

St DOMINIC

D for SAINT DOMINIC, Spanish by birth,
Who shone like a star in all parts of the earth.
In France there were heretics called Albigenses
Who poisoned the Faith with their lying pretences,
And spread their ridiculous nonsense about ;
But Saint DOMINIC went and soon hunted them out.
Then with Lawrence and Bertrand and Peter Cellani
He started his Order of *Dominicani*,
Or *Domini Canes*, the Dogs of the LORD,
Who go hunting for souls in the might of the Word.
The MASTER they follow in black-and-white coat
To catch men by the heart instead of the throat.
Our LADY much loved this dear Knight of the LORD
And her Rosary served for his Buckler and Sword.

SAINT EDMUND *of* CANTERBURY, *Bishop and Confessor;*
Born at Abingdon, about 1170; *Archbishop of Canterbury,* 1234;
Died, 1240. *Feast, November* 16.

St EDMUND

E for SAINT EDMUND; at Oxford one day
After school he went out in the meadows to play,
And a little white Figure stood by him and cried,
"Don't you know me, dear EDMUND, your friend and your
guide?
I am with you by day, I am with you by night,
When you sleep, when you wake, when you read, when you write."
On his forehead four letters proclaimed the Good News,*
"This is JESUS of NAZARETH, King of the Jews."
EDMUND lived to be Primate of England, and died
On the throne Saint AUGUSTINE had once occupied.

* I.N.R.I.

SAINT FRANCIS of ASSISI, *Confessor; Founder of the Order of Friars Minor, called Grey Friars; also of the "Poor Clares" or Second Order Franciscan, and of the Third Order, for the Laity; Born at Assisi, 1182; Died at St. Mary of the Angels, October 3, 1226. Feasts, October 4 and September 17 (Impression of the Stigmata).*

St FRANCIS *of* ASSISI

For FRANCIS of ASSISI, Poet and GOD'S Troubadour,
Martyr to his love for JESUS, truest lover of the poor.
Once he saw up in the trees a crowd of merry little birds,
So he preached a sermon to them, and they listened to his words :
"Praise the LORD, my little sisters, for the LORD your GOD is good ;
In the Ark that NOE made He saved your fathers from the Flood."
Pleased because he called them "sisters," all the birds spread out
their wings
And flew down to Brother Francis, who could say such pretty things.
"Praise the LORD, my little sisters, for the LORD your GOD is good,
And He gives you trees for houses, streams for drink, and grain for food."
Then they stretched their necks and bowed their heads until they touched
the sod,
While he told them they must "study always to give praise to GOD."
Lastly with the Cross he blessed them, and their faith the birds confessed,
Flying off in four battalions, North and South and East and West.
Out of all the lovely deeds that FRANCIS did at sweet Assisi
I have chosen only this, because its lesson is so easy :
"Praise the LORD, and love His creatures, birds and beasts as well
as men."
Sweet Saint FRANCIS of ASSISI, would that he were here again.

SAINT GREGORY *the* GREAT, *Pope, Confessor, Doctor of the Church; Born in Rome,* 540; *Pope* 590 *to* 604. *Feast, March* 12.

St GREGORY *the* GREAT

G is for GREGORY the GREAT, who walked about the town
Of Rome, and found the English slaves on sale for half-a
crown ;
"Why have these boys blue eyes," he asked, when ours have eyes
of brown ?"
When he heard that they were Angles, and that Alla was their king,
He said, "In the land of Alla, Alleluia they shall sing ;
For we'll make the Angles Angels by the message that we'll bring."
Saint AUGUSTINE went to Angleland for Pope Saint GREGORY,
And converted our poor ancestors to Christianity ;
And that is why both you and I are Christians, don't you see ?

SAINT HELEN, *Empress, Widow, Mother of the Emperor Constantine; Born in England, perhaps at Colchester, about 245; Died in Rome, 328. Feast, August 18.*

St HELEN

H for SAINT HELEN, the Empress who sailed
To find the True Cross, on which JESUS was nailed.
When she set out from Rome she was eighty, but still
In the strength of her faith she reached Calvary Hill;
Where at last, with much digging and delving, she found
Three crosses exactly alike in the ground.
To a woman in pain the three crosses were brought
To see by which cross her relief would be wrought;
In vain were the first and the second applied,
On which the two Robbers had been crucified;
But when the third touched her the woman was healed,
And thus the True Cross of our LORD was revealed.

    This British Princess who was Empress at Rome,
    Was born, so they say, in a Colchester home;
    As she may have been born there, I think it's a pity
    Saint HELEN'S forgotten in Colchester City.

SAINT IGNATIUS *of* LOYOLA, *Confessor, Founder of the Society of Jesus, or Jesuits; Born at Loyola, in Spain, 1491; Died in Rome, 1556. Feast, July 31.*

St IGNATIUS

I for IGNATIUS, a brave Spanish Knight,
Who was wounded and had to retire from the fight;
He asked for a book that would answer his needs,
Some book about battles and chivalrous deeds,
But they gave him the Lives of the Saints which he read
From beginning to end as he lay ill in bed;
And when he had finished, he vowed and he swore
That he'd follow the Saints and be worldly no more.
No longer a soldier, he rose from his bed
And enlisted an Army for JESUS instead.

SAINT JEROME, *Priest, Confessor, and Doctor of the Church; born in Dalmatia, 346; Died at Bethlehem, 420. Feast, September 30.*

St JEROME

J for SAINT JEROME, a learned old Priest,
Who left his own country to live in the East.
One day as he walked in the desert he saw
A lion that limped with a thorn in its paw;
So he pulled out the thorn, and the lion, content
With his doctor and friend, went wherever he went.
The birds loved him too; with the lion and them
He lived in the stable at sweet Bethlehem,
    And there where our LORD and His Mother once trod
He translated the Bible that tells us of GOD.

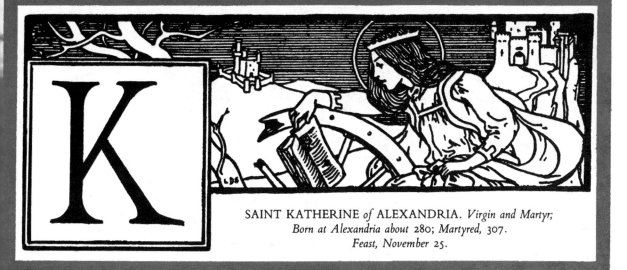

SAINT KATHERINE *of* ALEXANDRIA. *Virgin and Martyr;*
Born at Alexandria about 280; *Martyred,* 307.
Feast, November 25.

St KATHERINE

K for SAINT KATHERINE, Martyr, you see ;
She was learned and lovely and good as could be ;
She knew mathematics, and learnt how to speak
And to read and to write both in Latin and Greek.
She once had a vision that JESUS, her King,
Came and made her His Own with a gold wedding-ring.
Soon after this vision, King Maximin came
And offered her marriage and riches and fame :
" I'll make you my Empress, if you will deny
The name of CHRIST JESUS—if not, you shall die."
" I will die," she replied ; and was tied to a wheel
That was all covered over with razors of steel ;
But the lightning destroyed it, so Maximin said,
" Take her out of the city and cut off her head."
Saint KATHERINE'S body by Angels was carried
To Sinai's summit, where MOSES had tarried ;
A Martyr and Virgin, she wears the gold ring
She received from CHRIST JESUS, the Heavenly King.

SAINT LOUIS, *King of France, Confessor, Penitent of the Third Order of Saint Francis. Born at Poissy, in France, 1215; Died in Northern Africa, 1270. Feast, August 25.*

St LOUIS

L for SAINT LOUIS, a King without blame,
Who ruled over France as the Ninth of his name.
When LOUIS was given the Crown made of Thorn
Which CHRIST on the Cross of His Passion had worn,
He carried that Most Holy Crown in his hand
From Sens into Paris, barefoot through the land ;
Then he got a small piece of the True Cross as well,
And built for these relics *La Sainte Chapelle.*
Now LOUIS fell ill, and they thought he was dead,
But he suddenly rose with new strength from his bed,
And resolving to fight the good fight for our LORD,
Put on his chain-armour, took helmet and sword,
And asked the Archbishop of Paris to bless
The Cross of Crusade that he sewed on his dress.
    In the crown of a King and the Habit and Cord
    Of Saint FRANCIS he died, and was crowned by the LORD.

SAINT MARTIN *of* TOURS, *Bishop and Confessor; called Apostle of Gaul; Born in Pannonia,* 316; *Founded the first French Monastery, near Poitiers,* 360; *Bishop of Tours,* 372; *Died,* 396.
Feast, November 11.

St MARTIN

M for SAINT MARTIN, in Mitre and Cope
(The Bishop of Tours, not Saint MARTIN the Pope);
His father, a soldier, disliked and despised
The True Faith, and prevented his being baptized
By making him serve in the army of Gaul,
Though he wasn't that sort of a soldier at all.
At Amiens one day, in the wind and the sleet,
He was stopped by a beggar who begged in the street;
He'd no money to give, so he made a great tear
In his cloak and gave part to the beggar to wear.
That night in a vision Saint MARTIN was shown
Our LORD as He reigns on His heavenly Throne;
He was wearing the piece that the beggar had worn!
For CHRIST takes what we give to the poor and forlorn.

SAINT NORBERT, *Bishop and Confessor, Founder,* A.D. 1119,
*of the Premonstratensians (Pré montré means Meadow shown), or
White Canons, sometimes called Norbertines; born at Cologne,* 1065;
Died May 6, 1134. *Feast, June 6.*

St NORBERT

N for SAINT NORBERT, a man of Cologne,
Who was friends with the Emperor then on the throne;
He lived the gay life of a courtier—I mean
He was *not* quite so good as he ought to have been.
He was hunting one day, when a thunderbolt fell
And reminded this courtier of Judgement and Hell.
Resolving that he would be worldly no more,
He sold his possessions to give to the poor,
And set out like a sower to sow the good seed
In a land overgrown with heretical weed.
A number of people abandoned the world
To serve under the banner Saint NORBERT unfurled;
For our LADY designed him a habit of white
(Like the ANGELS') and *Showed* him a *Meadow,* the site
Where, in loving accord with our LADY'S intentions,
He built the first House of the Premonstratensians.

SAINT ODO, *Abbot of Cluny, Confessor; Born in Aquitaine, France; Abbot of Cluny, 927; Died 942. Feast, November 18.*

St ODO

O is ODO, son of Obbo, by his mother consecrated
To Saint MARTIN, for the Cloister to be strictly educated ;
But his father took and placed him with the Count of Aquitaine,
Where he spent his time in hawking and in other sports profane ;
But he suffered from bad headaches, which his father felt quite sure
Meant Saint MARTIN was offended, so he sent him off to Tours.
His vocation was undoubted, for his holiness increased,
So they sent him on to Paris to prepare to be a Priest.
At Paris, as he went to Mass one bitter winter's day
He gave his warm fur mantle to a beggar by the way ;
As he wasn't rich enough to buy another in its stead,
He soon became so frozen that he had to go to bed ;
But when he snuggled in the sheets, all shivering with cold,
What should he find beneath them but a shining piece of gold !
  ODO lived to be an Abbot, and was very very strict
  For the Cluniac Observance of the Rule of BENEDICT.

SAINT PHILIP NERI, *Confessor, called "Apostle of Rome,"*
Founder of the Congregation of the Oratory; Born at Florence,
July 21, 1515; Died in Rome, 1595. Feast, May 26.

St PHILIP NERI

P is good SAINT PHILIP NERI, friend of all the friends of Rome
He was eighteen when he chose the Holy City for his home ;
There he lived the life of hermits, eating little else but bread,
In one tiny little room in which he never had a bed.
PHILIP had the gifts and graces of Saint PETER and Saint PAUL,
And the Romans turned to piety and penance at his call,
While the numberless young people who sought PHILIP for advice
Said his humble little room was like an earthly Paradise.
He longed to die for CHRIST, as in the Catacomb he prayed
At the grave in which the Martyr, Saint SEBASTIAN, was laid ;
A Martyr's death is glorious, but PHILIP has the glory
Of founding a great Congregation, called the Oratory.
　　If I told you half the holy things that PHILIP did and said,
　　I should have to end the Alphabet with "P" instead of "Z.'

SAINT QUENTIN, *Martyr; Died at St. Quentin, in France,*
286. *Feast, October* 31.

St QUENTIN

Q for SAINT QUENTIN, who suffered in Gaul
Such tortures, I cannot describe them at all ;
(You see in the picture he carries two spits,
Which the torturers used when they pulled him to bits).
No threats could deter, and no promises win him ;
He openly spoke of the faith that was in him,
And perished, commending his soul to the LORD,
Who has promised the Martyr eternal reward.
His body was found in the river by chance,
And his name is still borne by a City in France.

SAINT RICHARD, *Bishop of Chichester, Confessor; Born, near Worcester, 1197; Died at Dover, 1253. Feast, April 3.*

St RICHARD

R for SAINT RICHARD, who, so it is said,
Subsisted at Oxford on porridge and bread.
Saint EDMUND, the holy Archbishop, befriended
Young Richard de Wych, when his studies were ended ;
And GOD worked a wonder—*I* think so at least—
When this excellent man was ordained as a Priest ;
For the oil of anointing, the sign of GOD'S grace,
Burst out of the vessel all over his face.
As Bishop Saint RICHARD won every man's love,
Being wise as the serpent and meek as the dove.
Having preached a crusade all along the south side
Of the country, at last, while at Dover, he died.
Though wicked King Harry long after pulled down
The Shrine of his body in Chichester town,
And took all the gold and the jewels, they say
The King left us his bones, and they lie there to-day ;
So when you're at Chichester, whisper a prayer
To Saint RICHARD, whose relics are, probably, there.

SAINT SEBASTIAN, *Martyr, called Lay Apostle; Born at Narbonne, about 265; Went to Rome in 284; Martyred at Rome about 288. Feast, January 20.*

St SEBASTIAN

S for SEBASTIAN bound to a tree,
And riddled with arrows by Cæsar's decree ;
When they loosed him he fell, and they thought he was slain,
But he rose and appeared before Cæsar again ;
At length he was cruelly cudgelled to death,
Confessing his LORD with his very last breath.
A soldier who strove for no earthly renown,
Twice he fought a good fight, and GOD gave him a Crown.

SAINT THOMAS *of* CANTERBURY, *Bishop and Martyr, Born in London, December 21, 1118; Consecrated Archbishop of Canterbury 1152; Martyred, 1166. Feast, December 29.*

St THOMAS

Tis also a Martyr, SAINT THOMAS I mean,
The bravest Archbishop that ever was seen.
Saint THOMAS was Primate of England, and fought
For the rights of the Church which the King set at nought ;
So they quarrelled, these two, for a very long time,
Until Henry the Second committed this crime :—
He threatened Saint THOMAS'S death, or at least
He said, "Who will *get rid* of this pestilent Priest ?"
FitzUrse and De Morville and Richard Le Breton
And William De Tracey, who heard the King threaten,
Rode off to the Abbey of CHRIST Church in Kent
And slew the good Priest the King called "pestilent,"
On the last day but two in the month of December—
A date which all Englishmen used to remember,
Till Harry the Eighth, who had made himself Pope,*
Broke Saint THOMAS'S statues in Mitre and Cope ;
Yet still, where at Lambeth his empty niche stands,
Thames bargemen salute him with reverent hands.

* *"He would be the King, the whole King, and nothing but the King; he would be the Pope, the whole Pope, and something more than the Pope."*—STUBBS.

SAINT URSULA *and her Companions, Virgins and Martyrs;*
Died at Cologne, 451; Commemorated on October 21.

St URSULA

U is URSULA the Virgin, whom GOD told to leave her home
With a company of Virgins on a pilgrimage to Rome;
They crossed the Alps barefooted into Italy from Gaul
And visited the thresholds of Saint PETER and Saint PAUL;
Then back again they started, but a band of cruel Huns
Made a company of Martyrs of that company of Nuns.
The last to die was URSULA, and lo! a wondrous grace
Shone round her as she went to meet her SAVIOUR face to face.
Perhaps some day you'll go and pay a visit to Cologne,
Where Saint URSULA was martyred and her relics are still shown.

SAINT VINCENT *of* PAUL, *Confessor, Founder of the Congregation of the Mission, and of the Sisters of Charity; Born at Puy, in Gascony, France, April 24, 1576; Died in Paris, September 27, 1660. Feast, July 19.*

St VINCENT *of* PAUL

V is a Frenchman, SAINT VINCENT of PAUL,
Who served as a slave to the Turks first of all ;
No Saint is impatient, wherever he be,
But probably VINCENT prayed hard to be free,
Till GOD had compassion on him in his pain
And brought him back safe to his country again.
There he founded an Order of Sisters ; perhaps
You have seen them in London, with large flapping caps ?
They look after the poor and the sick, all for love,
While Saint VINCENT prays for them in Heaven above.

SAINT WILFRID *of* YORK, *Bishop and Confessor; Born about* 634;
Bishop of Lindisfarne, 664; *of York,* 666; *and Selsey,* 687;
Died, 709. *Feast, October* 12.

St WILFRID *of* YORK

W'S WILFRID, in Mitre and Cope,
Who appealed like a Catholic straight to the Pope,
And said when the people rebelled at his yoke
That Saint PETER knew better than North-Country folk.
In Yorkshire he raised a poor child from the dead
And gave him safe back to his mother instead;
He taught them to fish down in Sussex, and then
He ordained them as Priests to be Fishers of Men.
His life was much better than your life, or mine,
And he died in the year seven hundred and nine.

SAINT XYSTUS, *Pope and Martyr. Pope from September, 255, to his Martyrdom in 258. Feast, August 11.*

St XYSTUS

X for SAINT XYSTUS, a very old man,
Who was Pope when a great persecution began.
He had a young Deacon, Saint LAWRENCE, and they
Were both carried off to the Judges one day ;
Some cowards to idols and sprites sacrificed,
But XYSTUS and LAWRENCE were faithful to CHRIST,
For though they were tortured they wouldn't give in,
But chose rather to die than commit such a sin ;
    And so they were able their courage to keep,
    And like the GOOD SHEPHERD both died for the Sheep.

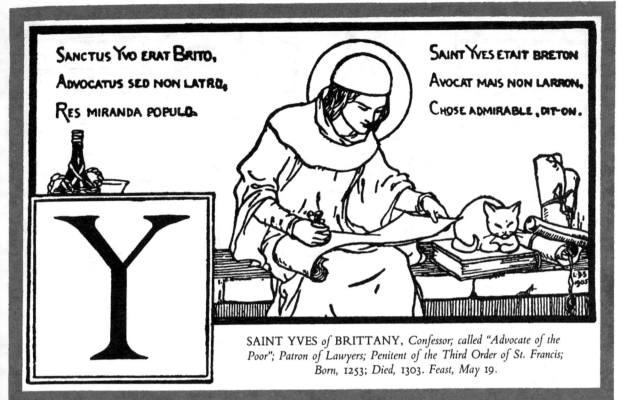

Sanctus Yvo erat Brito,
Advocatus sed non latro,
Res miranda populo.

Saint Yves était breton
Avocat mais non larron,
Chose admirable, dit-on.

SAINT YVES *of* BRITTANY, *Confessor; called "Advocate of the Poor"; Patron of Lawyers; Penitent of the Third Order of St. Francis; Born, 1253; Died, 1303. Feast, May 19.*

St YVES

Sanctus Yvo erat Brito,
Advocatus sed non latro,
Res miranda populo.

Saint Yves était breton,
Avocat mais non larron,
Chose admirable, dit-on.

Y for a Lawyer, as good as pure gold
When Lawyers were not always good, we are told.
SAINT YVES as an Advocate at the Assize
Defended the weak and confounded the "wise."
He looked upon wealth as a terrible curse,
Though you see in the picture he carries a purse;
But this means that he used what he had in good measure,
And is also a sign of his heavenly treasure;
For he never took money for services given,
Preferring to lay up his treasure in Heaven.
He died in the year thirteen hundred and three,
A priest and a lawyer as good as can be,
And still pleads for his clients in both these professions,
An Advocate still at the Heavenly Sessions.

SAINT ZITA, *Virgin; Born about* 1210; *Lived for forty-eight years in the service of one Fatinelli, citizen of Lucca, Italy; Died,* 1272. *Feast, April* 27.

St ZITA

Z for SAINT ZITA, the good kitchen-maid ;
She prayed, and she prayed, and she prayed, and she prayed ;
One morning she got so absorbed in her prayers,
She simply neglected her household affairs.
Too late she remembered 'twas bread-making day,
And she trembled to think what her mistress would say.
She flew to the oven, looked in it, and cried,
" Glory be to the LORD ! the bread's ready inside ! "
The Angels had kneaded it, raised it with yeast,
Made the fire, put the pans in the oven—at least
I can only suppose that was how it was done,
For the bread was all baked by a quarter to one.
        To pray like Saint ZITA, but not to be late,
        Is the way to be good, and (if possible) great.

Three men with the pen and one man with the paints
Have depicted the lives of these
twenty-six SAINTS

" Make Friends with the SAINTS, for the SAINTS are
GOD'S Friends " ℂ Is the MORAL
with which the SAINTS'
ALPHABET
ENDS

Neumann Press